# Super Easy Carnivore Diet Cookbook

**2000 Days of Quick & Delicious Recipes for Beginners with a 30-Day Meal Plan to Achieve Weight Loss, Increase Energy & Mental Clarity, Reduce Inflammation, and Stabilize Blood Sugar Levels**

Savoring Healthy Living Without Compromising Taste

**Julianna Wiggins**

# TABLE OF CONTENTS

# INTRODUCTION

Dear readers,

Julianna Wiggins, a distinguished chef and a luminary in the domain of nutritious cuisine, specializes in crafting Carnivore Diet recipes. Her deep-seated passion for this unique culinary approach, combined with her expertise in its health benefits, marks Julianna as a leading figure in the sphere of health-focused gastronomy.

Julianna's recipes are a fusion of robust flavors, crafted meticulously to enhance wellness while ensuring each meal remains deliciously satisfying. She embodies the principle of relishing food while adhering to a health-conscious diet, and her enthusiasm permeates her culinary creations.

Her professional and personal journey in perfecting the Carnivore Diet is driven by both passion and experience. Understanding the complexities and challenges associated with adopting this lifestyle, Julianna uses her own transformative culinary experiences to inspire and support others on their wellness journeys.

With her latest book, "Carnivore Diet Cookbook: 2000 Days of Delicious, Quick & Super Easy Recipes for Beginners," Julianna aims to revolutionize how we view health and diet. This comprehensive guide is designed to aid readers in achieving their health goals through a 30-day meal plan that focuses on weight loss, increased energy, mental clarity, reduced inflammation, and stabilized blood sugar levels.

With Julianna Wiggins as your culinary guide, diving into the Carnivore Diet becomes not just feasible, but a thrilling adventure filled with rich flavors and robust health.

# CHAPTER 1: FUNDAMENTALS OF THE CARNIVORE DIET

## What is the Carnivore Diet?

The Carnivore Diet is a dietary regimen that excludes almost all foods except for meat. It often includes fish, seafood, and sometimes other animal products such as eggs and certain dairy products. This diet is based on the belief that the human body is better adapted to consuming animal-derived foods and that eliminating plant-based foods can bring numerous health benefits.

Proponents of the Carnivore Diet claim that such a diet can aid in **weight loss, improve digestion, reduce inflammation, and even alleviate symptoms of certain conditions such as autoimmune disorders and diabetes**. However, it should be noted that scientific research supporting these claims is limited, and many health experts highlight the potential risks associated with this diet, including a lack of dietary fiber, vitamins, and minerals, as well as a possible increased risk of cardiovascular diseases due to high consumption of saturated fats.

**As with any significant change in diet, it is recommended to consult with a physician or a dietitian before starting the Carnivore Diet.**

## Nutritional Focus:

The Carnivore Diet provides a macronutrient profile rich in protein and fats, with virtually zero carbohydrates. This macronutrient distribution can lead to a state of ketosis, where the body, in the absence of carbs, begins to burn fat as its primary energy source. However, the diet's primary aim isn't necessarily to induce ketosis but to eliminate potential inflammatory agents derived from plant foods and processed products.

## Health Claims:

Advocates of the Carnivore Diet report numerous health benefits, including **weight loss, enhanced mental clarity, increased energy levels, reduced inflammation, improved digestion,** and alleviation of symptoms associated with various health conditions, such as **autoimmune diseases, diabetes, and digestive disorders**. While anecdotal evidence abounds, scientific research on the long-term effects and benefits of a strictly carnivorous diet is still in its nascent stages.

## Culinary Perspective:

From a culinary standpoint, the Carnivore Diet offers an opportunity to explore a vast array of cooking methods and cuts of meat, emphasizing the importance of quality and variety. It encourages the consumption of different animal proteins, including underutilized cuts and organ meats, which are packed with nutrients often lacking in a standard Western diet.

## Sustainability and Ethical Considerations:

Sustainability and ethical sourcing are critical considerations for many followers of the

Carnivore Diet. Advocates often emphasize the importance of choosing grass-fed, pasture-raised, and wild-caught animal products to ensure higher nutrient profiles and support sustainable farming and fishing practices.

## Conclusion:

The Carnivore Diet represents a radical departure from conventional dietary guidelines, advocating for a return to an ancestral way of eating focused solely on animal products. While it has garnered a growing following due to its purported health benefits, individuals considering this diet should do so with careful consideration of their health status, nutritional needs, and in consultation with healthcare professionals.

# Benefits of the Carnivore Diet

The Carnivore Diet, with its focus on animal-based foods, offers a range of potential benefits that have attracted a growing number of followers worldwide. Here's an exploration of the key advantages that proponents of this diet often report:

## Weight Loss and Body Composition

Many individuals turn to the Carnivore Diet for its potential to aid in weight loss and improve body composition. The high protein and fat content can enhance satiety, reducing overall calorie intake without the need for meticulous tracking. Additionally, the elimination of carbohydrates helps to stabilize blood sugar levels, reducing cravings and the likelihood of overeating.

## Enhanced Mental Clarity and Energy Levels

A significant number of carnivore dieters report experiencing heightened mental clarity and sustained energy levels. This could be attributed to the stable blood sugar levels and the absence of fluctuating energy highs and lows commonly associated with carb-heavy diets. The diet's focus on nutrient-dense foods may also play a crucial role in supporting cognitive function and energy metabolism.

## Reduction in Inflammation and Autoimmune Symptoms

The Carnivore Diet may offer therapeutic benefits for individuals with autoimmune conditions or chronic inflammation. By eliminating potential dietary triggers found in plant foods, such as lectins, gluten, and nightshades, many find relief from the symptoms of autoimmune disorders and a noticeable reduction in inflammatory markers.

## Digestive Health

An unexpected benefit for many on the Carnivore Diet is improved digestive health. The elimination of fiber and complex carbohydrates, which can be difficult for some people to digest, often results in reduced bloating, gas, and other gastrointestinal discomforts. The diet's simplicity allows the gut to heal and can be particularly beneficial for those with conditions like IBS or SIBO.

## Simplicity and Ease

The Carnivore Diet is lauded for its simplicity. With no need to count calories, measure portions, or navigate complicated food lists, meal preparation becomes straightforward and

# Nutrient Sources and Recommended Daily Intakes on the Carnivore Diet

| Nutrient | Recommended Daily Intake for Men | Recommended Daily Intake for Women | Carnivore Diet Sources |
|---|---|---|---|
| Vitamin A | 900 mcg | 700 mcg | Beef liver, cod liver |
| Vitamin B1 (Thiamine) | 1.2 mg | 1.1 mg | Pork, beef, liver |
| Vitamin B2 (Riboflavin) | 1.3 mg | 1.1 mg | Liver, eggs, meat |
| Vitamin B3 (Niacin) | 16 mg NE | 14 mg NE | Tuna, beef liver, chicken |
| Vitamin B5 (Pantothenic Acid) | 5 mg | 5 mg | Liver, beef, chicken |
| Vitamin B6 (Pyridoxine) | 1.3-1.7 mg | 1.3-1.5 mg | Turkey, beef, tuna |
| Vitamin B7 (Biotin) | 30 mcg | 30 mcg | Eggs, liver, salmon |
| Vitamin B9 (Folate) | 400 mcg | 400 mcg | Beef liver, eggs |
| Vitamin B12 (Cobalamin) | 2.4 mcg | 2.4 mcg | Meat, fish, shellfish, liver |
| Iron | 8 mg | 18 mg / 8 mg | Beef liver, oysters, beef |
| Zinc | 11 mg | 8 mg | Meat, shellfish, cheese |

These food items are excellent sources of the respective nutrients within the carnivore diet framework. However, the amount of each food needed to meet the daily requirements can vary based on the specific food item and its preparation method. It's always recommended to consult with a healthcare professional to tailor the diet to individual needs.

# CHAPTER 2: 30-DAY MEAL PLAN

| Day | Breakfast (625 kcal) | Lunch (875 kcal) | Snack (375 kcal) | Dinner (625 kcal) |
|---|---|---|---|---|
| Day 1 | Bacon-Wrapped Chicken Thighs - p.24 | Pulled Pork and Bacon Bowl with Duck Fat Dressing - p.38 | Crispy Bacon Chips - p.51 | Spicy Chicken Wings - p.63 |
| Day 2 | Poached Eggs over Ground Lamb - p.28 | Whole Grilled Chicken in the Oven - p.41 | Fish Pancakes - p.53 | New York Strip Steak with Clarified Butter - p.69 |
| Day 3 | Smoked Salmon and Cream Cheese Roll-Ups - p.33 | Chicken Cutlets with Cheese - p.40 | Carnivore Pancakes with Meat Filling - p.53 | Grilled Swordfish - p.74 |
| Day 4 | Ground Beef and Chorizo Hash - p.24 | Meatballs with Bechamel Sauce - p.39 | Turkey Bacon Roll-Ups - p.52 | Classic Ribeye Steak with Salt Crust - p.69 |
| Day 5 | Beef Liver Steak - p.32 | Pork Chops and Bacon Stew - p.46 | Bacon-Wrapped Egg Cups - p.55 | Beef Porterhouse with Herb Infused Lard - p.71 |
| Day 6 | Seared Tuna Steaks with Herb Butter - p.34 | Chicken Stewed in Ginger-Soy Sauce - p.42 | Spicy Beef Jerky - p.52 | Pulled Pork Shoulder with Crispy Fat - p.67 |
| Day 7 | Turkey and Egg Breakfast Casserole - p.29 | Turkey Thigh and Heart Bowl with Turkey Drippings - p.40 | Pork Rind Nachos (No Carbs) - p.51 | Grilled Salmon with Lemon Butter - p.72 |
| Day 8 | Pan-Seared Duck Breast with Berry Reduction - p.26 | Duck Breast and Liver Salad with Duck Fat Vinaigrette - p.41 | Chicken Liver and Egg Bites - p.56 | Pork Shank Braised in Beef Broth - p.66 |
| Day 9 | Grilled Heart Skewers with Chimichurri Sauce - p.30 | Beef Rib Stew - p.45 | Pork Belly and Egg Mini Pies (No Flour) - p.55 | Filet Mignon with Crispy Beef Bacon - p.70 |
| Day 10 | Scallop and Bacon Skewers - p.37 | Bacon-Wrapped Beef Fillet with Egg Yolk Glaze - p.48 | Carnivore Moussaka - p.54 | Salted Beef Tenderloin with Pork Lard Béarnaise - p.66 |
| Day 11 | Egg-Wrapped Meat Tacos (No Tortilla) - p.28 | Zrazy - Meat Rolls with Eggs - p.50 | Duck Fat Hollandaise - p.57 | Grilled T-Bone Steak with Bone Marrow Butter - p.70 |
| Day 12 | Lamb Chops with Rosemary and Garlic - p.26 | Chopped Lamb Shoulder Bowl with Lamb Fat Dressing - p.39 | Pork Lard Chimichurri - p.58 | Mackerel Fillets with Crispy Skin - p.72 |
| Day 13 | Spicy Shrimp Omelette - p.34 | Pulled Pork Shoulder Soup - p.46 | Turkey and Egg Mini Quiches (No Crust) - p.56 | Turkey Breast Roulade with Pork Fat - p.68 |

| Day | Breakfast (625 kcal) | Lunch (875 kcal) | Snack (375 kcal) | Dinner (625 kcal) |
|---|---|---|---|---|
| Day 14 | Pork Belly Bites with Spicy Dipping Sauce - p.25 | Prosciutto-Wrapped Chicken Thighs with Liver Pate Spread - p.48 | Creamy Bacon Fat Aioli - p.57 | Seared Scallops with Pork Belly Crumbs - p.74 |
| Day 15 | Marinated Beef Tongue Slices with Horseradish Cream - p.30 | Chicken Fillet in Cream with Cheese - p.45 | Bacon Fat and Black Pepper Marinade - p.61 | Spiced Turkey Legs (Carnivore Style) - p.65 |
| Day 16 | Crab Meat Scrambled Eggs - p.35 | Ham-Wrapped Pork Loin with Cheese Filling - p.49 | Beef Tallow Bearnaise - p.58 | Crispy Chicken Cutlets (Pork Rind Crusted) - p.67 |
| Day 17 | Grilled Sardines with Lemon Butter - p.33 | Meat Rolls "Palchiki" - p.50 | Duck Fat and Thyme Marinade - p.59 | Herring Steaks with Dill Butter - p.75 |
| Day 18 | Pork Sausages with Mustard Glaze - p.27 | Chicken Thigh and Liver Soup - p.47 | Salt-Cured Pork Belly - p.54 | Baked Salmon with Herb Crust (Carnivore Style) - p.73 |
| Day 19 | Smoked Haddock with Poached Egg - p.37 | Turkey Breast and Liver Stew - p.47 | Chicken Schmaltz and Lemon Marinade - p.60 | Shrimp Scampi (Carnivore Style) - p.75 |
| Day 20 | Pan-Seared Chicken Liver with Onions - p.31 | Pulled Pork and Bacon Bowl with Duck Fat Dressing - p.38 | Fish Fat and Lemon Zest Marinade - p.62 | Pork Chop with Crispy Pork Belly Crust - p.64 |
| Day 21 | Poached Eggs over Ground Lamb - p.28 | Oven-Baked Chicken Tabaka with Crispy Skin - p.43 | Turkey Bacon Roll-Ups - p.52 | Sirloin Steak with Beef Tallow Drizzle - p.71 |
| Day 22 | Butter Poached Cod with Dill - p.36 | Beef Rib Stew - p.45 | Pork Belly and Egg Mini Pies (No Flour) - p.55 | Grilled Swordfish - p.74 |
| Day 23 | Smoked Salmon and Cream Cheese Roll-Ups - p.33 | Chicken Stewed in Ginger-Soy Sauce - p.42 | Carnivore Moussaka - p.54 | Beef Brisket with Smoked Sea Salt - p.63 |
| Day 24 | Ground Beef and Chorizo Hash - p.24 | Turkey Thigh and Heart Bowl with Turkey Drippings - p.40 | Bacon-Wrapped Egg Cups - p.55 | Grilled Salmon with Lemon Butter - p.72 |
| Day 25 | Pork Belly Bites with Spicy Dipping Sauce - p.25 | Meatballs with Bechamel Sauce - p.39 | Spicy Beef Jerky - p.52 | Duck Breast with Crispy Skin - p.64 |
| Day 26 | Seared Tuna Steaks with Herb Butter - p.34 | Pulled Pork Shoulder Soup - p.46 | Turkey and Egg Mini Quiches (No Crust) - p.56 | Filet Mignon with Crispy Beef Bacon - p.70 |
| Day 27 | Marinated Beef Tongue Slices with Horseradish Cream - p.30 | Chicken Cutlets with Cheese - p.40 | Duck Fat Hollandaise - p.57 | Pork Shank Braised in Beef Broth - p.66 |

| Day | Breakfast (625 kcal) | Lunch (875 kcal) | Snack (375 kcal) | Dinner (625 kcal) |
|---|---|---|---|---|
| Day 28 | Bacon-Wrapped Chicken Thighs - p.24 | Chopped Lamb Shoulder Bowl with Lamb Fat Dressing - p.39 | Pork Rind Nachos (No Carbs) - p.51 | Beef Porterhouse with Herb Infused Lard - p.71 |
| Day 29 | Lamb Chops with Rosemary and Garlic - p.26 | Whole Grilled Chicken in the Oven - p.41 | Chicken Liver and Egg Bites - p.56 | Spiced Turkey Legs (Carnivore Style) - p.65 |
| Day 30 | Grilled Heart Skewers with Chimichurri Sauce - p.30 | Bacon-Wrapped Beef Fillet with Egg Yolk Glaze - p.48 | Creamy Bacon Fat Aioli - p.57 | Classic Ribeye Steak with Salt Crust - p.69 |

**Note:** This 30-day meal plan is designed for 2,500 calories per day across 4 meals. The distribution of 2,500 calories across four meals on the carnivore diet can vary depending on your preferences and schedule. However, it's important to ensure balance so that each meal is satisfying and nutritious. Here's one of the possible ways to distribute the calories:

**Breakfast:** 25% of the total calorie intake - approximately 625 calories. Breakfast might include a steak or eggs with bacon, providing a good mix of proteins and fats to start the day.

**Lunch:** 35% of the total calorie intake - approximately 875 calories. Lunch could consist of a larger portion of meat, such as roast beef or beef ribs, possibly with a piece of butter added to increase the fat content.

**Snack:** 15% of the total calorie intake - approximately 375 calories. The snack can be light but nutritious, for example, a small portion of fatty meat or a few pieces of cheese if you include dairy products in your diet.

**Dinner:** 25% of the total calorie intake - approximately 625 calories. Dinner might contain a variety of proteins, such as fish or chicken, possibly with the addition of some fats in the form of an animal fat sauce.

These proportions are not strict rules, and you can adapt them according to your needs and preferences. It's important to listen to your body's signals and adjust the portion sizes and macronutrient ratios to feel your best.

**Important:** The greens and all carbohydrate products shown in the photos are used solely for decorative purposes and aesthetic satisfaction. Please follow the recipe to see which ingredients you should use.

# CHAPTER 3: BREAKFASTS: Energizing Meat-Based Breakfasts

## Bacon-Wrapped Chicken Thighs

**Prep: 10 minutes | Cook: 25 minutes | Serves: 1**

**Ingredients:**

- 1 chicken thigh, boneless and skinless (150g)
- 2 strips of bacon (70g)
- Salt and pepper to taste

**Instructions:**

1. Preheat your oven to 400°F (200°C).
2. Season the chicken thigh with salt and pepper.
3. Wrap the chicken thigh with the bacon strips, securing with toothpicks if necessary.
4. Place on a baking sheet and bake in the preheated oven until the chicken is cooked through and the bacon is crispy, about 20-25 minutes.

**Nutritional Facts (Per Serving):** Calories: 625 | Sugars: 0g | Fat: 47g | Carbohydrates: 0g | Protein: 48g | Fiber: 0g | Sodium: 900mg | Vitamin A: 0µg | Vitamin B1: 0.1mg | Vitamin B2: 0.2mg | Vitamin B3: 11mg | Vitamin B5: 1mg | Vitamin B6: 0.6mg | Vitamin B7: 0µg | Vitamin B9: 5µg | Vitamin B12: 0.9µg | Iron: 2.1mg | Zinc: 3.8mg

## Ground Beef and Chorizo Hash

**Prep: 10 minutes | Cook: 20 minutes | Serves: 1**

**Ingredients:**

- 4 oz ground beef (113g)
- 2 oz chorizo (57g)
- Salt and pepper to taste

**Instructions:**

1. Heat a skillet over medium-high heat.
2. Add the ground beef and chorizo. Break the meat apart with a spoon. Cook until browned and no pink remains, about 10-12 minutes.
3. Season with salt and pepper to taste. Serve hot.

**Nutritional Facts (Per Serving):** Calories: 625 | Sugars: 0g | Fat: 48g | Carbohydrates: 0g | Protein: 48g | Fiber: 0g | Sodium: 875mg | Vitamin A: 0µg | Vitamin B1: 0.1mg | Vitamin B2: 0.2mg | Vitamin B3: 8mg | Vitamin B5: 0.9mg | Vitamin B6: 0.5mg | Vitamin B7: 0µg | Vitamin B9: 10µg | Vitamin B12: 2.4µg | Iron: 3mg | Zinc: 5.5mg

## Pork Belly Bites with Spicy Dipping Sauce

**Prep: 15 minutes | Cook: 40 minutes | Serves: 1**

### Ingredients:

- Pork belly cubes (200g)
- 1 tbsp olive oil (15ml)
- Salt and pepper to taste

**For the Spicy Dipping Sauce:**
- 2 tbsp apple cider vinegar (30ml)
- 1 tsp hot chili flakes (5g)
- 1 tsp honey (5ml) (optional for those who consume minimal sugar)

### Instructions:

1. Preheat the oven to 425°F (220°C).
2. Toss pork belly cubes with olive oil, salt, and pepper.
3. Spread on a baking sheet and roast until crisp, about 30-40 minutes, turning halfway through.
4. For the sauce, mix apple cider vinegar, hot chili flakes, and honey (if using) in a small bowl.
5. Serve pork belly bites with the spicy dipping sauce on the side.

**Nutritional Facts (Per Serving):** Calories: 625 | Sugars: 1g (Optional) | Fat: 55g | Carbohydrates: 1g (Optional) | Protein: 35g | Fiber: 0g | Sodium: 200mg | Vitamin A: 0µg | Vitamin B1: 0.6mg | Vitamin B2: 0.3mg | Vitamin B3: 11mg | Vitamin B5: 1.3mg | Vitamin B6: 0.4mg | Vitamin B7: 0µg | Vitamin B9: 5µg | Vitamin B12: 1.2µg | Iron: 1.8mg | Zinc: 4mg

## Sausage and Bacon Skillet Fry-Up

**Prep: 5 minutes | Cook: 15 minutes | Serves: 1**

### Ingredients:

- 2 pork sausages (150g)
- 2 slices of bacon (60g)
- Salt and pepper to taste

### Instructions:

1. Heat a skillet over medium-high heat.
2. Add the sausages and bacon to the skillet. Cook the sausages for about 10 minutes, turning occasionally until evenly browned and cooked through.
3. Cook the bacon until crisp, about 5 minutes, then transfer both to a plate.
4. Season with salt and pepper to taste.

**Nutritional Facts (Per Serving):** Calories: 625 | Sugars: 0g | Fat: 50g | Carbohydrates: 1g | Protein: 42g | Fiber: 0g | Sodium: 1,350mg | Vitamin A: 0µg | Vitamin B1: 0.7mg | Vitamin B2: 0.3mg | Vitamin B3: 10mg | Vitamin B5: 1.5mg | Vitamin B6: 0.4mg | Vitamin B7: 0µg | Vitamin B9: 5µg | Vitamin B12: 2µg | Iron: 2.5mg | Zinc: 4mg

## Lamb Chops with Rosemary and Garlic

**Prep: 5 minutes | Cook: 10 minutes | Serves: 1**

**Ingredients:**

- 2 lamb chops (200g)
- 1 tsp chopped fresh rosemary (1g)
- 1 garlic clove, minced (3g)
- 1 tbsp olive oil (15ml)
- Salt and pepper to taste

**Instructions:**

1. Rub the lamb chops with olive oil, garlic, rosemary, salt, and pepper.
2. Heat a skillet over medium-high heat. Add the lamb chops and cook for about 4-5 minutes per side for medium-rare.
3. Let the chops rest for a few minutes before serving.

**Nutritional Facts (Per Serving):** Calories: 625 | Sugars: 0g | Fat: 48g | Carbohydrates: 1g | Protein: 47g | Fiber: 0g | Sodium: 75mg | Vitamin A: 0µg | Vitamin B1: 0.2mg | Vitamin B2: 0.4mg | Vitamin B3: 10mg | Vitamin B5: 1mg | Vitamin B6: 0.3mg |

## Pan-Seared Duck Breast with Berry Reduction

**Prep: 5 minutes | Cook: 20 minutes | Serves: 1**

**Ingredients:**

- 1 duck breast (200g)
- 1/4 cup mixed berries (frozen or fresh) (37g)
- 1 tsp balsamic vinegar (5ml)
- Salt and pepper to taste

**Instructions:**

1. Score the skin of the duck breast and season both sides with salt and pepper.
2. Heat a pan over medium heat and place the duck breast skin-side down. Cook for about 6-7 minutes until the skin is crisp.
3. Flip the breast and cook for another 5-6 minutes for medium-rare. Remove and let it rest.
4. In the same pan, add berries and balsamic vinegar. Cook until the berries break down and the sauce reduces to a glaze.
5. Slice the duck and serve with the berry reduction.

**Nutritional Facts (Per Serving):** Calories: 625 | Sugars: 4g | Fat: 45g | Carbohydrates: 5g | Protein: 52g | Fiber: 1g | Sodium: 220mg | Vitamin A: 155µg | Vitamin B1: 0.5mg | Vitamin B2: 0.6mg | Vitamin B3: 14mg | Vitamin B5: 1.7mg | Vitamin B6: 0.6mg | Vitamin B7: 0µg | Vitamin B9: 13µg | Vitamin B12: 5µg | Iron: 3mg | Zinc: 5mg

## Pork Sausages with Mustard Glaze

**Prep: 5 minutes | Cook: 20 minutes | Serves: 1**

### Ingredients:

- 2 pork sausages (200g)
- 1 tbsp mustard (15ml)
- 1 tsp honey (5ml)
- 1 tbsp olive oil (15ml)

### Instructions:

1.In a skillet, heat olive oil over medium heat. Add sausages and cook until browned and cooked through, turning occasionally, about 15 minutes.
2. Mix mustard and honey in a small bowl. Brush the mixture over the sausages during the last 5 minutes of cooking.

**Nutritional Facts (Per Serving):** Calories: 625 | Sugars: 5g | Fat: 49g | Carbohydrates: 5g | Protein: 35g | Fiber: 0g | Sodium: 1200mg | Vitamin A: 0µg | Vitamin B1: 0.7mg | Vitamin B2: 0.3mg | Vitamin B3: 9mg | Vitamin B5: 0.9mg | Vitamin B6: 0.4mg | Vitamin B7: 0µg | Vitamin B9: 4µg | Vitamin B12: 2µg | Iron: 2.5mg | Zinc: 3mg

## Crispy Pork Cracklings with Apple Cider Vinegar Dip

**Prep: 5 minutes | Cook: 1 hour | Serves: 1**

### Ingredients:

- 4 oz pork skin (cut into strips) (113g)
- 1/4 cup apple cider vinegar for dipping (60ml)
- Salt to taste

### Instructions:

1. Preheat your oven to 350°F (180°C).
2. Place pork skin strips on a baking sheet. Season with salt.
3. Bake for about 1 hour or until crispy and golden.
4. Serve with apple cider vinegar on the side for dipping.

**Nutritional Facts (Per Serving):** Calories: 625 | Sugars: 0g | Fat: 45g | Carbohydrates: 0g | Protein: 58g | Fiber: 0g | Sodium: 100mg | Vitamin A: 0µg | Vitamin B1: 0.2mg | Vitamin B2: 0.2mg | Vitamin B3: 11mg | Vitamin B5: 1.2mg | Vitamin B6: 0.3mg | Vitamin B7: 0µg | Vitamin B9: 5µg | Vitamin B12: 0.8µg | Iron: 2mg | Zinc: 4mg

## Meatballs with Bechamel Sauce

**Prep: 20 minutes | Cook: 30 minutes | Serves: 1**

### Ingredients:

- 3.5 oz ground pork (100g)
- 3.5 oz ground turkey (100g)
- 1 egg
- 1/4 cup grated cheese (30g)
- Salt and black pepper to taste

**Bechamel Sauce:**
- 1 tbsp butter (15g)
- 1 tbsp all-purpose flour (8g)
- 1 cup milk (240ml)
- Salt and nutmeg to taste

### Instructions:

1. Preheat the oven to 375°F (190°C).
2. In a bowl, combine ground pork, ground turkey, egg, grated cheese, salt, and pepper. Mix well.
3. Form the mixture into meatballs and place them in a baking dish.
4. To make the bechamel sauce, melt butter in a saucepan over medium heat. Add flour and stir constantly for 1 minute. Gradually add milk, stirring continuously until the sauce thickens. Season with salt and a pinch of nutmeg.
5. Pour the bechamel sauce over the meatballs.
6. Bake in the preheated oven for 30 minutes until the meatballs are cooked through and the sauce is bubbly.

**Nutritional Facts (Per Serving):** Calories: 875 | Sugars: 0g | Fat: 65g | Carbohydrates: 5g | Protein: 60g | Fiber: 0g | Sodium: 800mg | Vitamin A: 500µg | Vitamin B1: 0.3mg | Vitamin B2: 0.4mg | Vitamin B3: 10mg | Vitamin B5: 1mg | Vitamin B6: 0.7mg | Vitamin B7: 10µg | Vitamin B9: 20µg | Vitamin B12: 2.5µg | Iron: 3mg | Zinc: 6mg

## Chopped Lamb Shoulder Bowl with Lamb Fat Dressing

**Prep: 10 minutes | Cook: 1 hour | Serves: 1**

### Ingredients:

- 6 oz lamb shoulder, chopped (170g)
- 1 tbsp lamb fat (15ml)
- Salt and pepper to taste

### Instructions:

1. Season the chopped lamb shoulder with salt and pepper.
2. Roast or braise the lamb until tender, then chop into bite-sized pieces.
3. Warm the lamb fat and drizzle over the chopped lamb before serving.

**Nutritional Facts (Per Serving):** Calories: 875 | Sugars: 0g | Fat: 70g | Carbohydrates: 0g | Protein: 60g | Fiber: 0g | Sodium: 300mg | Vitamin A: 0µg | Vitamin B1: 0.1mg | Vitamin B2: 0.2mg | Vitamin B3: 10mg | Vitamin B5: 0.7mg | Vitamin B6: 0.6mg | Vitamin B7: 0µg | Vitamin B9: 20µg | Vitamin B12: 2.5µg | Iron: 4mg | Zinc: 7mg

## Chicken Cutlets with Cheese

**Prep 15 minutes | Cook: 20 minutes | Serves: 1**

### Ingredients:

- 14 oz ground chicken (400g)
- 1 egg
- 2 oz hard cheese, cubed (60g)
- Salt and black pepper to taste
- 3 tbsp corn oil (45ml) for frying

### Instructions:

1. In a bowl, combine ground chicken, egg, salt, and pepper. Mix well and knead for 5-10 minutes.
2. Form small patties from the mixture. Place cheese cubes in the center of each patty and seal.
3. Heat corn oil in a skillet over medium heat. Fry the cutlets on one side until golden brown, about 5-7 minutes.
4. Flip the cutlets and cook the other side until golden brown and the cheese is melted, about 5-7 minutes.

**Nutritional Facts (Per Serving):** Calories: 875 | Sugars: 0g | Fat: 65g | Carbohydrates: 1g | Protein: 60g | Fiber: 0g | Sodium: 600mg | Vitamin A: 400µg | Vitamin B1: 0.4mg | Vitamin B2: 0.5mg | Vitamin B3: 12mg | Vitamin B5: 1.2mg | Vitamin B6: 0.8mg | Vitamin B7: 15µg | Vitamin B9: 50µg | Vitamin B12: 2.5µg | Iron: 3mg | Zinc: 6mg

## Turkey Thigh and Heart Bowl with Turkey Drippings

**Prep: 10 minutes | Cook: 1 hour 30 minutes | Serves: 1**

### Ingredients:

- 6 oz turkey thigh (170g)
- 2 oz turkey heart (57g)
- 2 tbsp turkey drippings (30ml)
- Salt and pepper to taste

### Instructions:

1. Season the turkey thigh and heart with salt and pepper.
2. Roast or braise the thigh until tender, then chop into bite-sized pieces. Cook the heart until tender.
3. Drizzle turkey drippings over the thigh and heart before serving.

**Nutritional Facts (Per Serving):** Calories: 875 | Sugars: 0g | Fat: 65g | Carbohydrates: 0g | Protein: 70g | Fiber: 0g | Sodium: 300mg | Vitamin A: 0µg | Vitamin B1: 0.2mg | Vitamin B2: 0.3mg | Vitamin B3: 10mg | Vitamin B5: 1.5mg | Vitamin B6: 0.6mg | Vitamin B7: 0µg | Vitamin B9: 10µg | Vitamin B12: 3µg | Iron: 4mg | Zinc: 6mg

## Duck Breast and Liver Salad with Duck Fat Vinaigrette

**Prep: 10 minutes | Cook: 20 minutes | Serves: 1**

### Ingredients:

- 4 oz duck breast (113g)
- 2 oz duck liver (57g)
- 2 tbsp duck fat (30ml)
- 1 tbsp vinegar (15ml)
- Salt and pepper to taste

### Instructions:

1. Season the duck breast and liver with salt and pepper.
2. Pan-sear the duck breast skin-side down until crispy, then flip and cook to desired doneness. Sear the liver until cooked through.
3. Slice the duck breast and liver, and arrange on a plate. Mix duck fat and vinegar, and drizzle over the duck as a dressing.

**Nutritional Facts (Per Serving):** Calories: 875 | Sugars: 0g | Fat: 70g | Carbohydrates: 0g | Protein: 65g | Fiber: 0g | Sodium: 300mg | Vitamin A: 500µg | Vitamin B1: 0.3mg | Vitamin B2: 0.4mg | Vitamin B3: 15mg | Vitamin B5: 3mg | Vitamin B6: 0.7mg | Vitamin B7: 0µg | Vitamin B9: 60µg | Vitamin B12: 20µg | Iron: 8mg | Zinc: 5mg

## Whole Grilled Chicken in the Oven

**Prep: 10 minutes | Cook: 1 hour | Serves: 4**

### Ingredients:

- 1 whole chicken (4 lbs / 1800g)
- 1 packet chicken seasoning (30g)
- Salt and pepper to taste

### Instructions:

1. Preheat the oven to 350°F (180°C).
2. Rinse the chicken thoroughly and remove any remaining organs. Pat dry with paper towels.
3. Rub the chicken all over with the chicken seasoning, salt, and pepper.
4. Place the chicken on the oven rack and position a baking tray underneath to catch the drippings.
5. If your oven has a grill function, select it. Otherwise, set the oven to 350°F (180°C) and roast for 1 hour. Optionally, you can use the convection setting for a more even cook.

**Nutritional Facts (Per Serving):** Calories: 875 | Sugars: 0g | Fat: 65g | Carbohydrates: 0g | Protein: 70g | Fiber: 0g | Sodium: 500mg | Vitamin A: 700µg | Vitamin B1: 0.3mg | Vitamin B2: 0.4mg | Vitamin B3: 14mg | Vitamin B5: 1mg | Vitamin B6: 1mg |

Vitamin B7: 15µg | Vitamin B9: 30µg | Vitamin B12: 1.5µg | Iron: 2mg | Zinc: 4mg

## Chicken Stewed in Ginger-Soy Sauce

**Prep: 15 minutes | Cook: 25 minutes | Serves: 1**

### Ingredients:

- 10.5 oz chicken pieces (300g)
- 1 tbsp olive oil (15ml)
- 1 tbsp honey (20g)
- 2 tbsp soy sauce (30ml)
- 1 tbsp mustard with seeds (15g)
- 1/2 lemon, juiced
- 4 cloves garlic, minced
- 1 tsp grated fresh ginger (5g)
- Salt and pepper to taste

### Instructions:

1.Heat a skillet over medium-high heat. Place chicken pieces skin side down and cook for 5-6 minutes until crispy.

2. Add olive oil, flip the chicken, and cook for another 5 minutes until browned.

3. Mix garlic, ginger, mustard, lemon juice, honey, and soy sauce in a bowl. Pour over chicken.

4. Season with salt and pepper. Bring to a boil, reduce heat, and simmer for 10-15 minutes until the chicken is cooked through and the sauce thickens.

**Nutritional Facts (Per Serving):** Calories: 875 | Sugars: 10g | Fat: 45g | Carbohydrates: 12g |

Protein: 75g | Fiber: 0g | Sodium: 1000mg | Vitamin A: 100µg | Vitamin B1: 0.2mg | Vitamin B2: 0.3mg | Vitamin B3: 15mg | Vitamin B5: 1.5mg | Vitamin B6: 0.9mg | Vitamin B7: 0µg | Vitamin B9: 15µg | Vitamin B12: 2.7µg | Iron: 4.5mg | Zinc: 6mg

## Roast Duck

**Prep: 20 minutes | Cook: 1 hour 30 minutes | Serves: 4**

### Ingredients:

- 1 whole duck (4 lbs / 1800g)
- 3 apples, sliced (600g)
- 1 tbsp sea salt (15g)
- 1 tsp Provence herbs (5g)
- 4 cloves garlic, minced
- 1 tbsp mustard (15g)
- 2 tbsp sour cream (30ml)
- 2 tbsp soy sauce (30ml)

### Instructions:

1. Preheat oven to 350°F (180°C).

2. Rub duck with sea salt, Provence herbs, and minced garlic. Place in a roasting bag and refrigerate for 1 hour.

3. Stuff duck with sliced apples and sew the cavity shut.

4. Seal the duck in the roasting bag and roast for 1 hour.

5. Remove duck from the bag, brush with soy sauce, sour cream, and mustard mixture.

6. Roast uncovered for an additional 20-30 minutes until crispy and cooked to an internal temperature

of 165°F (74°C).

**Nutritional Facts (Per Serving):** Calories: 875 | Sugars: 0g | Fat: 65g | Carbohydrates: 10g | Protein: 55g | Fiber: 2g | Sodium: 1000mg | Vitamin A: 700µg | Vitamin B1: 0.3mg | Vitamin B2: 0.4mg | Vitamin B3: 12mg | Vitamin B5: 1mg | Vitamin B6: 0.9mg | Vitamin B7: 10µg | Vitamin B9: 20µg | Vitamin B12: 2.5µg | Iron: 4mg | Zinc: 6mg

## Oven-Baked Chicken Tabaka with Crispy Skin

**Prep: 20 minutes | Cook: 1 hour | Serves: 4**

### Ingredients:

- 1 whole chicken (2.6 lbs / 1200g)
- 2 tbsp Tkemali sauce or adjika (30ml)
- 3.5 oz butter, melted (100g)
- 1 tsp salt (5g)
- 1/2 tsp coriander (2.5g)
- 1/2 tsp fenugreek (2.5g)
- 1/2 tsp cayenne pepper (2.5g)
- 1/2 tsp dried garlic (2.5g)
- 1 tsp paprika (5g)

### Instructions:

1. Preheat the oven to 400°F (200°C).
2. Cut the chicken along the breastbone and spread it open. Remove the backbone and flatten the chicken.
3. Rinse the chicken under cold water and pat dry with paper towels. Cover with plastic wrap and pound to an even thickness.
4. Rub the chicken with Tkemali sauce or adjika and let it marinate for 15 minutes.
5. Melt the butter in the microwave and mix in the salt, coriander, fenugreek, cayenne pepper, dried garlic, and paprika.
6. Brush the butter and spice mixture all over the chicken.
7. Place the chicken on a rack in the oven with a baking tray underneath to catch the drippings. Roast until the chicken is golden brown and crispy, about 1 hour.

**Nutritional Facts (Per Serving):** Calories: 875 | Sugars: 0g | Fat: 65g | Carbohydrates: 1g | Protein: 65g | Fiber: 0g | Sodium: 600mg | Vitamin A: 700µg | Vitamin B1: 0.3mg | Vitamin B2: 0.4mg | Vitamin B3: 14mg | Vitamin B5: 1mg | Vitamin B6: 1mg | Vitamin B7: 15µg | Vitamin B9: 30µg | Vitamin B12: 1.5µg | Iron: 2mg | Zinc: 4mg

## Salt-Baked Chicken

**Prep: 10 minutes | Cook: 50 minutes | Serves: 4**

### Ingredients:

- 1 whole chicken (4 lbs / 1800g)
- 1 lemon
- 2 lbs coarse sea salt (900g)

# CHAPTER 11: SNACKS: Carnivore Snack Bites

## Crispy Bacon Chips

**Prep: 5 minutes | Cook: 20 minutes | Serves: 1**

### Ingredients:

- 6 slices bacon (180g)

### Instructions:

1. Preheat your oven to 400°F (200°C).
2. Line a baking sheet with parchment paper and arrange the bacon slices in a single layer.
3. Bake in the preheated oven until the bacon is crispy, about 15-20 minutes.
4. Transfer the bacon to a paper towel-lined plate to drain excess fat.
5. Once cooled, break into chip-sized pieces.

**Nutritional Facts (Per Serving):** Calories: 375 | Sugars: 0g | Fat: 30g | Carbohydrates: 0g | Protein: 25g | Fiber: 0g | Sodium: 1500mg | Vitamin A: 0µg | Vitamin B1: 0.1mg | Vitamin B2: 0.2mg | Vitamin B3: 8mg | Vitamin B5: 1mg | Vitamin B6: 0.4mg | Vitamin B7: 0µg | Vitamin B9: 2µg | Vitamin B12: 0.5µg | Iron: 1mg | Zinc: 2mg

## Pork Rind Nachos (No Carbs)

**Prep:5 minutes | Cook: 5 minutes | Serves: 1**

### Ingredients:

- 1 cup pork rinds (30g)
- 1/2 cup shredded cheddar cheese (50g)
- 1/4 cup diced jalapeños (30g)

### Instructions:

1. Preheat the oven to 350°F (175°C).
2. Arrange pork rinds on an oven-proof plate.
3. Sprinkle shredded cheese and diced jalapeños over the pork rinds.
4. Bake in the preheated oven until the cheese is melted, about 5 minutes.
5. Serve immediately.

**Nutritional Facts (Per Serving):** Calories: 375 | Sugars: 0g | Fat: 30g | Carbohydrates: 0g | Protein: 25g | Fiber: 0g | Sodium: 580mg | Vitamin A: 200µg | Vitamin B1: 0.1mg | Vitamin B2: 0.2mg | Vitamin B3: 4mg | Vitamin B5: 1mg | Vitamin B6: 0.2mg | Vitamin B7: 0µg | Vitamin B9: 5µg | Vitamin B12: 0.5µg | Iron: 0.5mg | Zinc: 2mg

## Spicy Beef Jerky

**Prep: 10 minutes (plus marinating) | Cook: 4 hours | Serves: 1**

### Ingredients:

- 4 oz beef, thinly sliced (113g)
- 1 tbsp soy sauce (15ml)
- 1 tsp chili flakes (5g)
- 1/2 tsp garlic powder (2.5g)
- 1/2 tsp onion powder (2.5g)

### Instructions:

1. In a bowl, mix soy sauce, chili flakes, garlic powder, and onion powder.
2. Add the beef slices to the marinade and ensure they are well coated. Marinate for at least 4 hours or overnight in the refrigerator.
3. Preheat the oven to 175°F (80°C).
4. Place the marinated beef slices on a wire rack over a baking sheet.
5. Dry in the oven for about 4 hours, or until the beef is dry and leathery. Allow to cool before eating.

**Nutritional Facts (Per Serving):** Calories: 375 | Sugars: 0g | Fat: 7g | Carbohydrates: 3g | Protein: 70g | Fiber: 0g | Sodium: 800mg | Vitamin A: 300µg | Vitamin B1: 0.1mg | Vitamin B2: 0.2mg | Vitamin B3: 25mg | Vitamin B5: 0.9mg | Vitamin B6: 0.6mg | Vitamin B7: 0µg | Vitamin B9: 5µg | Vitamin B12: 2.1µg | Iron: 8mg | Zinc: 10mg

## Turkey Bacon Roll-Ups

**Prep: 5 minutes | Cook: 10 minutes | Serves: 1**

### Ingredients:

- 4 slices turkey bacon (80g)
- 4 slices deli turkey breast (120g)

### Instructions:

1. Preheat a skillet over medium heat.
2. Cook the turkey bacon until it is partially cooked but still pliable, about 2-3 minutes per side.
3. Lay out the turkey breast slices. Place a slice of bacon on each and roll them up tightly.
4. Secure with toothpicks if necessary and return to the skillet.
5. Cook the roll-ups until the turkey breast is heated through and the bacon is crispy, about 5 minutes.

**Nutritional Facts (Per Serving):** Calories: 375 | Sugars: 0g | Fat: 22g | Carbohydrates: 0g | Protein: 42g | Fiber: 0g | Sodium: 1400mg | Vitamin A: 0µg | Vitamin B1: 0.1mg | Vitamin B2: 0.2mg | Vitamin B3: 8mg | Vitamin B5: 1.5mg | Vitamin B6: 0.6mg | Vitamin B7: 0µg | Vitamin B9: 10µg | Vitamin B12: 0.3µg | Iron: 1.5mg | Zinc: 2.5mg

## Carnivore Pancakes with Meat Filling

**Prep: 10 minutes | Cook: 20 minutes | Serves: 1**

### Ingredients:

- 2 large eggs
- 1/4 cup heavy cream (60ml)
- 1/2 lb ground beef (225g)
- 2 tbsp butter (30g)
- Salt and pepper to taste

### Instructions:

1. In a bowl, whisk eggs and heavy cream together.
2. Heat 1 tbsp butter in a non-stick skillet over medium heat. Pour half the egg mixture to form a thin pancake. Cook until set, about 2-3 minutes per side. Repeat with remaining batter.
3. In a separate skillet, brown the ground beef with salt and pepper until fully cooked, about 8-10 minutes.
4. Place the cooked beef onto the pancakes and roll them up.

**Nutritional Facts (Per Serving):** Calories: 375 | Sugars: 0g | Fat: 50g | Carbohydrates: 2g | Protein: 45g | Fiber: 0g | Sodium: 400mg | Vitamin A: 300µg | Vitamin B1: 0.1mg | Vitamin B2: 0.6mg | Vitamin B3: 5mg | Vitamin B5: 1mg | Vitamin B6: 0.4mg |

Vitamin B7: 20µg | Vitamin B9: 50µg | Vitamin B12: 3.5µg | Iron: 3mg | Zinc: 7mg

## Fish Pancakes

**Prep: 10 minutes | Cook: 10 minutes | Serves: 1**

### Ingredients:

- 5 egg whites (150g)
- 1/3 cup cooked fish, flaked (150g)
- 2 tbsp fat (30g)
- 1/2 cup grated cheese (100g)

### Instructions:

1. Blend egg whites, cooked fish, and fat until smooth. Season with spices if desired.
2. Pour the mixture onto a preheated non-stick skillet and cook for 3-4 minutes on one side.
3. Sprinkle grated cheese on one quarter of the pancake. Make a cut from the center to the edge of the pancake.
4. Fold the pancake over the cheese (1 over 2), then fold the remaining parts (3 over 2, and 4 under 2). Press gently with a spatula to melt the cheese.
5. Serve with sour cream and soft goat cheese.

**Nutritional Facts (Per Serving):** Calories: 3755 | Sugars: 0g | Fat: 45g | Carbohydrates: 2g | Protein:

50g | Fiber: 0g | Sodium: 300mg | Vitamin A: 200µg | Vitamin B1: 0.1mg | Vitamin B2: 0.3mg | Vitamin B3: 5mg | Vitamin B5: 0.5mg | Vitamin B6: 0.4mg | Vitamin B7: 10µg | Vitamin B9: 30µg | Vitamin B12: 2µg | Iron: 2mg | Zinc: 2mg

## Carnivore Moussaka

**Prep: 15 minutes | Cook: 40 minutes | Serves: 1**

### Ingredients:

- 1/4 lb veal, minced (115g)
- 1/4 lb lamb, minced (115g)
- 2 large eggs
- 1/2 cup grated Greek cheese (60g)
- 1 tbsp olive oil (15ml)
- Salt and pepper to taste

### Instructions:

1. Preheat oven to 350°F (175°C).
2. In a skillet, heat olive oil over medium heat. Brown the veal and lamb, seasoning with salt and pepper.
3. In a baking dish, layer the meat mixture and top with beaten eggs and grated cheese.
4. Bake for 30-35 minutes, until the top is golden and set.

**Nutritional Facts (Per Serving):** Calories: 375 | Sugars: 0g | Fat: 45g | Carbohydrates: 2g | Protein: 55g | Fiber: 0g | Sodium: 400mg | Vitamin A: 400µg | Vitamin B1: 0.1mg | Vitamin B2: 0.4mg | Vitamin B3: 5mg | Vitamin B5: 1mg | Vitamin B6: 0.4mg |

Vitamin B7: 20µg | Vitamin B9: 50µg | Vitamin B12: 3.5µg | Iron: 4mg | Zinc: 6mg

## Salt-Cured Pork Belly

**Prep: 15 minutes | Cook: 5 days (curing) | Serves: 10**

### Ingredients:

- 5 lbs pork belly with meat layers (2250g)
- 1/4 cup sea salt (60g)
- 2 tbsp black pepper (30g)
- 2 tbsp garlic (30g)
- 2 tbsp paprika (30g)

### Instructions:

1. Rub the pork belly with sea salt, black pepper, garlic, and paprika, ensuring even coverage.
2. Place the pork belly in a large container, cover, and refrigerate for 7 days. Turn the pork belly every day to ensure even curing.
3. After 5 days, rinse the pork belly under cold water to remove excess salt. Pat dry with paper towels.
4. Slice thinly to serve.

**Nutritional Facts (Per Serving):** Calories: 375 | Sugars: 0g | Fat: 35g | Carbohydrates: 0g | Protein: 15g | Fiber: 0g | Sodium: 800mg | Vitamin A: 500µg | Vitamin B1: 0.2mg | Vitamin B2: 0.2mg | Vitamin B3: 4mg | Vitamin B5: 0.5mg | Vitamin B6: 0.3mg | Vitamin B7: 5µg | Vitamin B9: 5µg | Vitamin B12: 1µg | Iron: 1.5mg | Zinc: 1.5mg

## Bacon-Wrapped Egg Cups

**Prep: 5 minutes | Cook: 20 minutes | Serves: 1**

### Ingredients:

- 3 slices bacon (90g)
- 2 large eggs (100g)
- Salt and pepper to taste

### Instructions:

1. Preheat the oven to 375°F (190°C).
2. Line each cup of a muffin tin with a slice of bacon, forming a ring.
3. Crack an egg into each bacon-lined cup.
4. Season with salt and pepper.
5. Bake in the preheated oven until the egg whites are set and yolks are cooked to your liking, about 15-20 minutes.
6. Carefully remove the egg cups from the tin and serve.

**Nutritional Facts (Per Serving):** Calories: 375 | Sugars: 0g | Fat: 30g | Carbohydrates: 1g | Protein: 25g | Fiber: 0g | Sodium: 600mg | Vitamin A: 240µg | Vitamin B1: 0.1mg | Vitamin B2: 0.5mg | Vitamin B3: 5mg | Vitamin B5: 1.4mg | Vitamin B6: 0.2mg | Vitamin B7: 10µg | Vitamin B9: 70µg | Vitamin B12: 0.9µg | Iron: 1.5mg | Zinc: 2mg

## Pork Belly and Egg Mini Pies (No Flour)

**Prep: 10 minutes | Cook: 20 minutes | Serves: 1**

### Ingredients:

- 100g pork belly, cut into small pieces
- 1 large egg (50g)
- Salt and pepper to taste

### Instructions:

1. Preheat your oven to 375°F (190°C).
2. Cook pork belly pieces in a pan until crispy.
3. Arrange the pork belly at the bottom of a small baking dish.
4. Crack the egg over the pork belly.
5. Season with salt and pepper.
6. Bake for 20 minutes or until the egg is set.

**Nutritional Facts (Per Serving):** Calories: 375 | Sugars: 0g | Fat: 30g | Carbohydrates: 0g | Protein: 20g | Fiber: 0g | Sodium: 330mg Vitamin A: 90µg | Vitamin B1 (Thiamine): 0.4mg | Vitamin B2 (Riboflavin): 0.2mg | Vitamin B3 (Niacin): 4.0mg | Vitamin B5 (Pantothenic Acid): 0.8mg | Vitamin B6 (Pyridoxine): 0.3mg | Vitamin B7 (Biotin): 5µg | Vitamin B9 (Folate): 24µg | Vitamin B12 (Cobalamin): 0.5µg | Iron: 1.2mg | Zinc: 2.2mg

150µg | Vitamin B1: 0.1mg | Vitamin B2: 0.2mg | Vitamin B3: 16mg | Vitamin B5: 0.9mg | Vitamin B6: 0.8mg | Vitamin B7: 0µg | Vitamin B9: 5µg | Vitamin B12: 2.4µg | Iron: 3mg | Zinc: 6mg

## Pulled Pork Shoulder with Crispy Fat

**Prep: 10 minutes | Cook: 6 hours | Serves: 1**

### Ingredients:

- 1 lb pork shoulder (450g)
- 1 tbsp salt (15g)
- 1 tsp black pepper (2g)

### Instructions:

1. Preheat your oven to 275°F (135°C).
2. Rub the pork shoulder all over with salt and black pepper.
3. Place the pork in a roasting pan, fat side up.
4. Slow roast in the oven until the meat is very tender and the fat is crispy, about 6 hours.

**Nutritional Facts (Per Serving):** Calories: 625 | Sugars: 0g | Fat: 45g | Carbohydrates: 0g | Protein: 55g | Fiber: 0g | Sodium: 1800mg | Vitamin A: 0µg | Vitamin B1: 1.2mg | Vitamin B2: 0.5mg | Vitamin B3: 15mg | Vitamin B5: 1.7mg | Vitamin B6: 0.8mg | Vitamin B7: 0µg | Vitamin B9: 5µg | Vitamin B12: 2.4µg | Iron: 3mg | Zinc: 5mg

## Crispy Chicken Cutlets (Pork Rind Crusted)

**Prep:10 minutes | Cook: 10 minutes | Serves: 1**

### Ingredients:

- 1 egg (50g)
- Salt and pepper to taste
- 1 chicken breast (200g)
- 1 cup crushed pork rinds (50g)

### Instructions:

1. Flatten the chicken breast to an even thickness using a meat mallet.
2. Season the chicken with salt and pepper.
3. Beat the egg in a shallow dish.
4. Place the crushed pork rinds in another shallow dish.
5. Dip the chicken breast first in the beaten egg, then coat thoroughly with the crushed pork rinds.
6. Heat a skillet with enough cooking oil to cover the bottom over medium heat.
7. Fry the chicken until golden brown and cooked through, about 5 minutes per side.
8. Drain on paper towels before serving.

**Nutritional Facts (Per Serving):** Calories: 625 | Sugars: 0g | Fat: 35g | Carbohydrates: 0g | Protein: 70g | Fiber: 0g | Sodium: 400mg | Vitamin A: 100µg | Vitamin B1: 0.1mg | Vitamin B2: 0.2mg | Vitamin B3: 16mg | Vitamin B5: 1mg | Vitamin B6: 0.6mg | Vitamin B7: 0µg | Vitamin B9: 10µg | Vitamin B12: 0.3µg | Iron: 2mg | Zinc: 2mg

## Turkey Breast Roulade with Pork Fat

**Prep: 15 minutes | Cook: 1 hour | Serves: 1**

**Ingredients:**

- 1 turkey breast, skinless and boneless (300g)
- 2 oz pork fat, thinly sliced (57g)

**Instructions:**

1. Preheat your oven to 350°F (175°C).
2. Lay the turkey breast flat on a cutting board. If thick, butterfly the breast to even thickness.
3. Season both sides with salt and pepper.
4. Lay slices of pork fat evenly across the turkey breast.
5. Roll the turkey breast tightly and tie with kitchen twine to secure.
6. Sear the roulade in a hot skillet on all sides until golden.
7. Transfer to the oven and roast until the internal temperature reaches 165°F (74°C), about 45 minutes.
8. Let rest for 10 minutes, remove twine, slice, and serve.

**Nutritional Facts (Per Serving):** Calories: 625 | Sugars: 0g | Fat: 35g | Carbohydrates: 0g | Protein: 75g | Fiber: 0g | Sodium: 600mg | Vitamin A: 0µg | Vitamin B1: 0.3mg | Vitamin B2: 0.4mg | Vitamin

B3: 25mg | Vitamin B5: 1.9mg | Vitamin B6: 1.5mg | Vitamin B7: 0µg | Vitamin B9: 20µg | Vitamin B12: 1.2µg | Iron: 3mg | Zinc: 6mg

## Turkey Drumsticks with Smoked Salt Crust

**Prep: 10 minutes | Cook: 1 hour 30 minutes | Serves: 1**

**Ingredients:**

- 2 turkey drumsticks (450g)
- 1 tbsp smoked salt (15g)
- 1 tsp black pepper (2g)

**Instructions:**

1. Preheat your oven to 375°F (190°C).
2. Pat the turkey drumsticks dry with paper towels.
3. Rub all over with smoked salt and black pepper.
4. Place the drumsticks on a baking sheet.
5. Roast in the preheated oven until the skin is crispy and the meat is tender, about 1.5 hours.

**Nutritional Facts (Per Serving):** Calories: 625 | Sugars: 0g | Fat: 35g | Carbohydrates: 0g | Protein: 70g | Fiber: 0g | Sodium: 2300mg | Vitamin A: 0µg | Vitamin B1: 0.1mg | Vitamin B2: 0.3mg | Vitamin B3: 8mg | Vitamin B5: 1.5mg | Vitamin B6: 1mg | Vitamin B7: 0µg | Vitamin B9: 10µg | Vitamin B12: 3µg | Iron: 4mg | Zinc: 7mg

# CHAPTER 16: DINNER: Steaks

## Classic Ribeye Steak with Salt Crust

**Prep: 5 minutes | Cook: 10 minutes | Serves: 1**

**Ingredients:**

- 1 ribeye steak (8 oz or 227g)
- 1 tbsp coarse sea salt (15g)

**Instructions:**

1. Preheat your grill or skillet over high heat.
2. Generously season both sides of the ribeye steak with coarse sea salt.
3. Place the steak on the grill or in the skillet and cook for about 5 minutes per side for medium-rare, or adjust the time for your preferred doneness.
4. Remove the steak from heat and let it rest for 5 minutes before serving to allow the juices to redistribute.

**Nutritional Facts (Per Serving):** Calories: 625 | Sugars: 0g | Fat: 45g | Carbohydrates: 0g | Protein: 52g | Fiber: 0g | Sodium: 2300mg | Vitamin A: 0µg | Vitamin B1: 0.1mg | Vitamin B2: 0.2mg | Vitamin B3: 14mg | Vitamin B5: 0.9mg | Vitamin B6: 0.7mg | Vitamin B7: 0µg | Vitamin B9: 4µg | Vitamin B12: 5.1µg | Iron: 4mg | Zinc: 10mg

## New York Strip Steak with Clarified Butter

**Prep: 5 minutes | Cook: 10 minutes | Serves: 1**

**Ingredients:**

- 1 New York strip steak (8 oz or 227g)
- 2 tbsp clarified butter (30ml)

**Instructions:**

1. Preheat your grill or skillet to high heat.
2. Season the steak with salt and pepper.
3. Sear the steak in the skillet or on the grill, using some of the clarified butter, about 5 minutes on each side for medium-rare.
4. Serve the steak topped with the remaining clarified butter melted over the top.

**Nutritional Facts (Per Serving):** Calories: 625 | Sugars: 0g | Fat: 50g | Carbohydrates: 0g | Protein: 42g | Fiber: 0g | Sodium: 200mg | Vitamin A: 130µg | Vitamin B1: 0.1mg | Vitamin B2: 0.2mg | Vitamin B3: 8mg | Vitamin B5: 0.7mg | Vitamin B6: 0.6mg | Vitamin B7: 0µg | Vitamin B9: 5µg | Vitamin B12: 1.2µg | Iron: 3mg | Zinc: 5mg

## Grilled T-Bone Steak with Bone Marrow Butter

**Prep: 5 minutes | Cook: 10 minutes | Serves: 1**

### Ingredients:

- 1 T-bone steak (12 oz or 340g)
- 2 tbsp bone marrow, rendered (30ml)

### Instructions:

1. Let the steak come to room temperature for 30 minutes before cooking.
2. Preheat your grill to high heat.
3. Season the T-bone steak generously with salt and pepper.
4. Grill the steak for about 5 minutes on each side for medium-rare.
5. In a small pan, gently warm the rendered bone marrow until it becomes liquid.
6. Pour the bone marrow butter over the steak just before serving.

**Nutritional Facts (Per Serving):** Calories: 625 | Sugars: 0g | Fat: 45g | Carbohydrates: 0g | Protein: 55g | Fiber: 0g | Sodium: 200mg | Vitamin A: 0µg | Vitamin B1: 0.1mg | Vitamin B2: 0.2mg | Vitamin B3: 15mg | Vitamin B5: 0.8mg | Vitamin B6: 0.6mg | Vitamin B7: 0µg | Vitamin B9: 5µg | Vitamin B12: 2.9µg | Iron: 4mg | Zinc: 12mg

## Filet Mignon with Crispy Beef Bacon

**Prep: 10 minutes | Cook: 15 minutes | Serves: 1**

### Ingredients:

- 1 filet mignon (200g)
- 3 slices of beef bacon (45g)

### Instructions:

1. Preheat your oven to 400°F (200°C).
2. Season the filet mignon with salt and pepper.
3. Wrap the filet tightly with slices of beef bacon.
4. Sear the bacon-wrapped filet on all sides in a hot skillet over medium-high heat until the bacon is crispy, about 3 minutes per side.
5. Transfer the skillet to the oven and cook to your desired doneness, approximately 5-7 minutes for medium-rare.
6. Rest the steak for 5 minutes before serving to allow the juices to redistribute.

**Nutritional Facts (Per Serving):** Calories: 625 | Sugars: 0g | Fat: 45g | Carbohydrates: 0g | Protein: 58g | Fiber: 0g | Sodium: 760mg | Vitamin A: 0µg | Vitamin B1: 0.15mg | Vitamin B2: 0.20mg | Vitamin B3: 14mg | Vitamin B5: 1.3mg | Vitamin B6: 0.6mg | Vitamin B7: 0µg | Vitamin B9: 12µg | Vitamin B12: 2.1µg | Iron: 4mg | Zinc: 5mg

## Sirloin Steak with Beef Tallow Drizzle

**Prep: 5 minutes | Cook: 10 minutes | Serves: 1**

### Ingredients:

- 1 sirloin steak (200g)
- Salt and pepper to taste
- 2 tbsp beef tallow, melted (30ml)

### Instructions:

1. Heat a grill or skillet over high heat.
2. Season the sirloin steak generously with salt and pepper.
3. Grill the steak to your preferred doneness, about 4-5 minutes per side for medium-rare.
4. Drizzle melted beef tallow over the steak just before serving for added richness.

**Nutritional Facts (Per Serving):** Calories: 625 | Sugars: 0g | Fat: 50g | Carbohydrates: 0g | Protein: 45g | Fiber: 0g | Sodium: 600mg | Vitamin A: 0µg | Vitamin B1: 0.1mg | Vitamin B2: 0.2mg | Vitamin B3: 10mg | Vitamin B5: 0.5mg | Vitamin B6: 0.4mg | Vitamin B7: 0µg | Vitamin B9: 8µg | Vitamin B12: 1.8µg | Iron: 3.5mg | Zinc: 4mg

## Beef Porterhouse with Herb Infused Lard

**Prep: 5 minutes | Cook: 15 minutes | Serves: 1**

### Ingredients:

- 1 porterhouse steak (350g)
- Salt and pepper to taste
- 2 tbsp lard, infused with herbs like rosemary and thyme (30ml)

### Instructions:

1. Let the steak sit at room temperature for 30 minutes before cooking.
2. Preheat your grill to high heat.
3. Season the porterhouse steak with salt and pepper.
4. Grill the steak, using some of the herb-infused lard to baste, about 7 minutes per side for medium-rare, depending on thickness.
5. Rest the steak for 5 minutes, then serve with a spoonful of the remaining herb-infused lard melted over the top.

**Nutritional Facts (Per Serving):** Calories: 625 | Sugars: 0g | Fat: 48g | Carbohydrates: 0g | Protein: 45g | Fiber: 0g | Sodium: 650mg | Vitamin A: 15µg | Vitamin B1: 0.2mg | Vitamin B2: 0.3mg | Vitamin B3: 13mg | Vitamin B5: 0.7mg | Vitamin B6: 0.5mg | Vitamin B7: 0µg | Vitamin B9: 10µg | Vitamin B12: 2.3µg | Iron: 4.2mg | Zinc: 6mg

# CHAPTER 17: DINNER: Seafood Dinners

## Grilled Salmon with Lemon Butter

**Prep: 5 minutes | Cook: 10 minutes | Serves: 1**

### Ingredients:

- 1 salmon steak (200g)
- 2 tbsp unsalted butter (30ml), melted
- 1 tbsp lemon juice (15ml)
- Salt and pepper to taste

### Instructions:

1. Preheat your grill to medium-high heat.
2. Season the salmon steak with salt and pepper.
3. Grill the salmon for about 5 minutes on each side, or until the fish flakes easily with a fork.
4. Mix the melted butter and lemon juice in a small bowl.
5. Pour the lemon butter over the grilled salmon just before serving.

**Nutritional Facts (Per Serving):** Calories: 625 | Sugars: 0g | Fat: 45g | Carbohydrates: 0g | Protein: 55g | Fiber: 0g | Sodium: 300mg | Vitamin A: 180µg | Vitamin B1: 0.15mg | Vitamin B2: 0.20mg | Vitamin B3: 11mg | Vitamin B5: 1.9mg | Vitamin B6: 0.9mg | Vitamin B7: 0µg | Vitamin B9: 15µg | Vitamin B12: 4.8µg | Iron: 1mg | Zinc: 0.7mg

## Mackerel Fillets with Crispy Skin

**Prep: 5 minutes | Cook: 8 minutes | Serves: 1**

### Ingredients:

- 2 mackerel fillets (200g)
- 1 tbsp olive oil (15ml)
- Salt and pepper to taste

### Instructions:

1. Heat olive oil in a non-stick skillet over medium-high heat.
2. Season the mackerel fillets with salt and pepper.
3. Place the fillets skin side down in the skillet.
4. Cook for about 4 minutes until the skin is crispy, then flip and cook for an additional 4 minutes or until done.
5. Serve immediately, skin side up.

**Nutritional Facts (Per Serving):** Calories: 625 | Sugars: 0g | Fat: 45g | Carbohydrates: 0g | Protein: 55g | Fiber: 0g | Sodium: 400mg | Vitamin A: 250µg | Vitamin B1: 0.3mg | Vitamin B2: 0.4mg | Vitamin B3: 12mg | Vitamin B5: 2mg | Vitamin B6: 1.2mg | Vitamin B7: 0µg | Vitamin B9: 10µg | Vitamin B12: 19µg | Iron: 2mg | Zinc: 1.3mg

## Sardine Skewers with Sea Salt

**Prep: 5 minutes | Cook: 5 minutes | Serves: 1**

### Ingredients:

- 10 sardines (200g), cleaned and gutted
- 1 tbsp sea salt (15g)
- Olive oil for brushing

### Instructions:

1. Preheat your grill to high heat.
2. Skewer the sardines and brush lightly with olive oil.
3. Sprinkle with sea salt.
4. Grill the skewers for about 2-3 minutes on each side or until the sardines are cooked through and slightly charred.
5. Serve hot off the grill.

**Nutritional Facts (Per Serving):** Calories: 625 | Sugars: 0g | Fat: 45g | Carbohydrates: 0g | Protein: 60g | Fiber: 0g | Sodium: 1500mg | Vitamin A: 150µg | Vitamin B1: 0.2mg | Vitamin B2: 0.3mg | Vitamin B3: 5mg | Vitamin B5: 1mg | Vitamin B6: 0.3mg | Vitamin B7: 0µg | Vitamin B9: 12µg | Vitamin B12: 8µg | Iron: 4mg | Zinc: 1.9mg

## Baked Salmon with Herb Crust (Carnivore Style)

**Prep: 10 minutes | Cook: 15 minutes | Serves: 1**

### Ingredients:

- 1 salmon fillet (200g)
- 1/4 cup crushed pork rinds (15g)
- 1 tbsp mixed dried herbs like dill and parsley (1g)
- Salt and pepper to taste

### Instructions:

1. Preheat your oven to 400°F (200°C).
2. Season the salmon fillet with salt and pepper.
3. In a small bowl, mix the crushed pork rinds with the dried herbs.
4. Press the pork rind and herb mixture onto the top of the salmon fillet to form a crust.
5. Place the salmon on a baking sheet lined with parchment paper.
6. Bake in the preheated oven for about 15 minutes, or until the salmon is cooked through and the crust is golden.

**Nutritional Facts (Per Serving):** Calories: 625 | Sugars: 0g | Fat: 45g | Carbohydrates: 0g | Protein: 60g | Fiber: 0g | Sodium: 200mg | Vitamin A: 50µg | Vitamin B1: 0.1mg | Vitamin B2: 0.2mg | Vitamin B3: 20mg | Vitamin B5: 2mg | Vitamin B6: 1mg | Vitamin B7: 0µg | Vitamin B9: 15µg | Vitamin B12: 5µg | Iron: 1mg | Zinc: 1mg

## Grilled Swordfish

**Prep: 10 minutes | Cook: 10 minutes | Serves: 1**

**Ingredients:**

- 1 swordfish steak (350g)
- 
- Salt and pepper to taste

**Instructions:**

1. Preheat your grill to high heat.
2. Rub the swordfish steak with olive oil and season with salt and pepper.
3. Grill the steak for about 5 minutes on each side or until the fish is cooked through and slightly charred.

**Nutritional Facts (Per Serving):** Calories: 625 | Sugars: 0g | Fat: 35g | Carbohydrates: 0g | Protein: 60g | Fiber: 0g | Sodium: 300mg | Vitamin A: 0µg | Vitamin B1: 0.1mg | Vitamin B2: 0.1mg | Vitamin B3: 15mg | Vitamin B5: 1mg | Vitamin B6: 0.5mg | Vitamin B7: 0µg | Vitamin B9: 10µg | Vitamin B12: 2mg | Iron: 1mg | Zinc: 1mg

## Seared Scallops with Pork Belly Crumbs

**Prep: 10 minutes | Cook: 10 minutes | Serves: 1**

**Ingredients:**

- 5 large sea scallops (200g)
- 2 oz pork belly, cooked and crumbled (57g)
- Salt and pepper to taste
- 1 tbsp olive oil (15ml)

**Instructions:**

1. Pat the scallops dry with a paper towel and season with salt and pepper.
2. Heat the olive oil in a skillet over high heat.
3. Sear the scallops for about 2 minutes on each side or until a golden crust forms.
4. Remove the scallops and briefly sauté the crumbled pork belly in the same skillet until crispy.
5. Serve the scallops topped with the crispy pork belly crumbs.

**Nutritional Facts (Per Serving):** Calories: 625 | Sugars: 0g | Fat: 45g | Carbohydrates: 0g | Protein: 55g | Fiber: 0g | Sodium: 650mg | Vitamin A: 0µg | Vitamin B1: 0.3mg | Vitamin B2: 0.1mg | Vitamin B3: 2mg | Vitamin B5: 1mg | Vitamin B6: 0.3mg | Vitamin B7: 0µg | Vitamin B9: 5µg | Vitamin B12: 1mg | Iron: 0.5mg | Zinc: 1mg

## Herring Steaks with Dill Butter

**Prep: 5 minutes | Cook: 10 minutes | Serves: 1**

### Ingredients:

- 2 herring steaks (200g)
- 2 tbsp unsalted butter (30ml), softened
- 1 tbsp fresh dill, finely chopped (1g)
- Salt and pepper to taste

### Instructions:

1. Preheat your grill or skillet over medium-high heat.
2. Season the herring steaks with salt and pepper.
3. Grill the herring steaks for about 3-4 minutes on each side until cooked through and lightly charred.
4. Mix the softened butter with chopped dill.
5. Top the hot herring steaks with dill butter just before serving, allowing it to melt over the fish.

**Nutritional Facts (Per Serving):** Calories: 625 | Sugars: 0g | Fat: 45g | Carbohydrates: 0g | Protein: 55g | Fiber: 0g | Sodium: 200mg | Vitamin A: 150µg | Vitamin B1: 0.1mg | Vitamin B2: 0.2mg | Vitamin B3: 15mg | Vitamin B5: 1mg | Vitamin B6: 0.5mg | Vitamin B7: 0µg | Vitamin B9: 15µg | Vitamin B12: 18µg | Iron: 2mg | Zinc: 1mg

## Shrimp Scampi (Carnivore Style)

**Prep: 5 minutes | Cook: 8 minutes | Serves: 1**

### Ingredients:

- 8 large shrimp, peeled and deveined (200g)
- 3 tbsp unsalted butter (45ml)
- Salt to taste

### Instructions:

1. Heat a skillet over medium-high heat.
2. Add butter to the skillet and melt until foamy.
3. Add the shrimp and sauté for about 2-3 minutes per side until pink and cooked through.
4. Season with salt and serve immediately, drizzling any remaining butter over the shrimp.

**Nutritional Facts (Per Serving):** Calories: 625 | Sugars: 0g | Fat: 45g | Carbohydrates: 0g | Protein: 60g | Fiber: 0g | Sodium: 500mg | Vitamin A: 500µg | Vitamin B1: 0.1mg | Vitamin B2: 0.2mg | Vitamin B3: 5mg | Vitamin B5: 1mg | Vitamin B6: 0.5mg | Vitamin B7: 0µg | Vitamin B9: 15µg | Vitamin B12: 2mg | Iron: 2.5mg | Zinc: 1.5mg

## Clam and Mussel Medley in Seafood Broth

**Prep: 10 minutes | Cook: 15 minutes | Serves: 1**

### Ingredients:

- 100g clams, cleaned
- 100g mussels, cleaned
- 1 cup seafood broth (250ml)
- Salt to taste

### Instructions:

1. In a large pot, bring the seafood broth to a simmer over medium heat.
2. Add the clams and mussels to the pot. Cover and cook until the shells open, about 5-7 minutes.
3. Discard any shells that do not open.
4. Season the broth with salt, and serve the shellfish in the broth, ensuring a generous amount of broth in each serving.

**Nutritional Facts (Per Serving):** Calories: 625 | Sugars: 0g | Fat: 45g | Carbohydrates: 0g | Protein: 60g | Fiber: 0g | Sodium: 800mg | Vitamin A: 100µg | Vitamin B1: 0.2mg | Vitamin B2: 0.3mg | Vitamin B3: 4mg | Vitamin B5: 1mg | Vitamin B6: 0.5mg | Vitamin B7: 0µg | Vitamin B9: 28µg | Vitamin B12: 12µg | Iron: 6mg | Zinc: 2mg

## Mackerel in Bone Broth

**Prep: 5 minutes | Cook: 20 minutes | Serves: 1**

### Ingredients:

- 2 mackerel fillets (200g)
- Salt to taste
- 2 cups beef bone broth (500ml)

### Instructions:

1. Pour the beef bone broth into a small saucepan and bring to a gentle simmer over medium heat.
2. Season the mackerel fillets with salt and gently place them in the simmering broth.
3. Poach the fillets in the broth for about 15-20 minutes, or until the fish is cooked through and tender.
4. Carefully remove the mackerel fillets from the broth with a slotted spoon and place them on a plate.
5. If desired, reduce the broth by simmering for an additional 5-10 minutes to concentrate the flavors, then pour it over the cooked mackerel as a sauce.

**Nutritional Facts (Per Serving):** Calories: 625 | Sugars: 0g | Fat: 45g | Carbohydrates: 0g | Protein: 60g | Fiber: 0g | Sodium: 300mg | Vitamin A: 50µg | Vitamin B1: 0.5mg | Vitamin B2: 0.4mg | Vitamin B3: 19mg | Vitamin B5: 1.2mg | Vitamin B6: 1mg | Vitamin B7: 0µg | Vitamin B9: 12µg | Vitamin B12: 18µg | Iron: 1.5mg | Zinc: 1mg

# CHAPTER 18: BONUSES

## Meal Plans and Shopping Templates: Streamlined tools to optimize your meal planning.

To elevate your experience with the Carnivore Diet, we've crafted a 30-day grocery shopping guide specifically tailored to our cookbook. This guide focuses on simplifying meal preparation by emphasizing high-quality animal products and minimizing processed foods. Be vigilant about hidden carbs and sugars, particularly in any processed meats or additives. Adjust quantities based on your dietary needs, adhering to the Carnivore Diet's focus on meat-based, high-protein, high-fat nutrients. Embark on a journey of simple, satisfying, and health-promoting eating!

## Grocery Shopping List for 7-Day Meal Plan

### Meat and Poultry:

2 lbs (900g) chicken thighs
2 lbs (900g) pulled pork
1 lb (450g) bacon
2 lbs (900g) chicken wings
1 lb (450g) ground lamb
1 whole chicken (3-4 lbs / 1.4-1.8kg)
1 lb (450g) chicken breasts
1 lb (450g) swordfish steak
1 lb (450g) ground beef
1 lb (450g) chorizo sausage
1 lb (450g) beef liver
1.5 lbs (680g) pork chops
1.5 lbs (680g) pork shoulder
1.5 lbs (680g) turkey breast
1 lb (450g) turkey thighs
1 lb (450g) turkey hearts
1.5 lbs (680g) ribeye steak
1.5 lbs (680g) porterhouse steak
1 lb (450g) New York strip steak

### Seafood:

1 lb (450g) smoked salmon
1 lb (450g) salmon fillets
1 lb (450g) tuna steaks

### Dairy and Fats:

1 dozen eggs
1 cup (240ml) heavy cream
1 lb (450g) butter
1/2 cup (120ml) duck fat
1/2 cup (120ml) clarified butter
1 cup (240ml) cream cheese
Cheese

### Herbs, Spices, and Seasonings:

Sea salt
Black pepper
Smoked sea salt
1 tbsp mustard
1 tbsp ground ginger
2 tbsp soy sauce
1 tsp dried thyme
1 tsp dried rosemary
1 tsp paprika
1 tsp garlic powder

### Other:

1 tbsp honey
2 tbsp olive oil

### Special Ingredients:

1 lemon
1/2 cup (120ml) Tkemali sauce (or adjika)

## Grocery Shopping List for 8-14 Day Meal Plan

### Meat and Poultry:

2 lbs (900g) duck breast
1 lb (450g) duck liver
1 lb (450g) chicken liver
2 lbs (900g) pork shank
1 lb (450g) beef heart
1.5 lbs (680g) beef ribs
1 lb (450g) pork belly
1.5 lbs (680g) beef fillet
1.5 lbs (680g) beef tenderloin
1 lb (450g) ground beef
1 lb (450g) pork loin
1 lb (450g) lamb chops

1 lb (450g) lamb shoulder
1.5 lbs (680g) T-bone steak
1 lb (450g) turkey breast
1 lb (450g) turkey thighs
1 lb (450g) turkey hearts
1 lb (450g) pork ribs
1 lb (450g) prosciutto
1 lb (450g) pork sausage

## Seafood:

1 lb (450g) scallops
1 lb (450g) shrimp
1 lb (450g) mackerel fillets

## Dairy and Fats:

1 dozen eggs
1 lb (450g) butter
1 cup (240ml) heavy cream
1/2 cup (120ml) duck fat
1/2 cup (120ml) pork lard
1 cup (240ml) cream cheese
Cheese

## Herbs, Spices, and Seasonings:

Sea salt
Black pepper
Smoked sea salt
1 tbsp mustard
1 tbsp ground ginger
2 tbsp soy sauce
1 tsp dried thyme
1 tsp dried rosemary
1 tsp paprika
1 tsp garlic powder
1 tbsp chimichurri sauce
1 tbsp Hollandaise sauce
1 tbsp Béarnaise sauce

## Other:

1 cup (240ml) beef broth
1/2 cup (120ml) chicken broth
1 tbsp honey

2 tbsp olive oil

## Special Ingredients:

1/2 cup (120ml) Tkemali sauce (or adjika)
2 tbsp bone marrow
1 lemon

## Grocery Shopping List for 15-21 Day Meal Plan

## Meat and Poultry:

1 lb (450g) beef tongue
1 lb (450g) chicken fillets
1.5 lbs (680g) turkey legs
1 lb (450g) crab meat
1 lb (450g) pork loin
1 lb (450g) chicken cutlets
1 lb (450g) sardines
1 lb (450g) pork sausages
1 lb (450g) chicken thighs
1 lb (450g) chicken liver
1 lb (450g) pork belly
1 lb (450g) salmon fillets
1 lb (450g) turkey breast
1 lb (450g) turkey liver
1 lb (450g) shrimp
1 lb (450g) pork chop
1 lb (450g) ground lamb
1 whole chicken (3-4 lbs / 1.4-1.8kg)
1 lb (450g) sirloin steak
1 lb (450g) bacon
Seafood:
1 lb (450g) haddock
1 lb (450g) herring

## Dairy and Fats:

1 dozen eggs
1 lb (450g) butter
1 cup (240ml) heavy cream
1/2 cup (120ml) duck fat

1/2 cup (120ml) pork lard
1 cup (240ml) cream cheese
Cheese

## Herbs, Spices, and Seasonings:

Sea salt
Black pepper
1 tbsp mustard
1 tbsp ground ginger
2 tbsp soy sauce
1 tsp dried thyme
1 tsp dried rosemary
1 tsp paprika
1 tsp garlic powder
1 tbsp chimichurri sauce
1 tbsp Hollandaise sauce
1 tbsp Béarnaise sauce
1 tbsp thyme marinade
1 tbsp lemon zest marinade
1 tbsp black pepper marinade

## Other:

1 cup (240ml) beef broth
1/2 cup (120ml) chicken broth
1 tbsp honey
2 tbsp olive oil

## Special Ingredients:

1/2 cup (120ml) Tkemali sauce (or adjika)
2 tbsp bone marrow
1 lemon

## Grocery Shopping List for 22-28 Day Meal Plan

## Meat and Poultry:

1 lb (450g) cod fillets
2 lbs (900g) beef ribs
1 lb (450g) pork belly

1 swordfish steak (200g)
1 lb (450g) smoked salmon
1 lb (450g) chicken thighs
1 lb (450g) ground beef
1 lb (450g) chorizo
2 lbs (900g) turkey thighs
1 lb (450g) turkey hearts
1 lb (450g) bacon
1 lb (450g) tuna steaks
2 lbs (900g) pulled pork shoulder
1 lb (450g) marinated beef tongue
1 lb (450g) chicken cutlets
1 lb (450g) lamb shoulder
2 lbs (900g) beef porterhouse steak
1 lb (450g) filet mignon
1 lb (450g) duck breast
1 lb (450g) beef brisket

## Dairy and Fats:

1 dozen eggs
1 cup (240ml) heavy cream
1/2 cup (120ml) butter

1/2 cup (120ml) cream cheese
1 cup (240ml) duck fat
1 cup (240ml) pork lard
Cheese

## Herbs, Spices, and Seasonings:

Sea salt
Black pepper
Dill
Spicy dipping sauce (pre-made or ingredients to make your own: chili powder, garlic, vinegar)
Herb butter (or ingredients to make your own: butter, mixed herbs)
Soy sauce
Ground ginger
Paprika
Béarnaise sauce (pre-made or ingredients to make your own: butter, egg yolks, vinegar, shallots, tarragon)

Hollandaise sauce (pre-made or ingredients to make your own: butter, egg yolks, lemon juice)
Horseradish cream (pre-made or ingredients to make your own: horseradish, cream)

## Other:

1 cup (240ml) beef broth
1 cup (240ml) chicken broth
1 tbsp olive oil
1 tbsp mustard
1 tbsp garlic powder

## Special Ingredients:

1/2 cup (120ml) Tkemali sauce (or adjika)
2 tbsp bone marrow
1 lemon
1 pack pork rinds